Test Color Page

Let your creativity soar
on the wings of
imagination.

LET'S START WITH SOMETHING EASY...

It is...

____

Paint your world with
the colors of your
heart.

REALLY EASY...

It is...

____

Paint your world with the colors of your heart.

REALLY EASY...

It is...

____

Embrace the canvas
and let your emotions
flow.

It is...

____

Embrace the canvas
and let your emotions
flow.

It is...

____

Colors have the power to bring joy to your soul.

It is...

____

Discover the magic
that lies within the
colors.

It is...

____

With every stroke, you create a masterpiece.

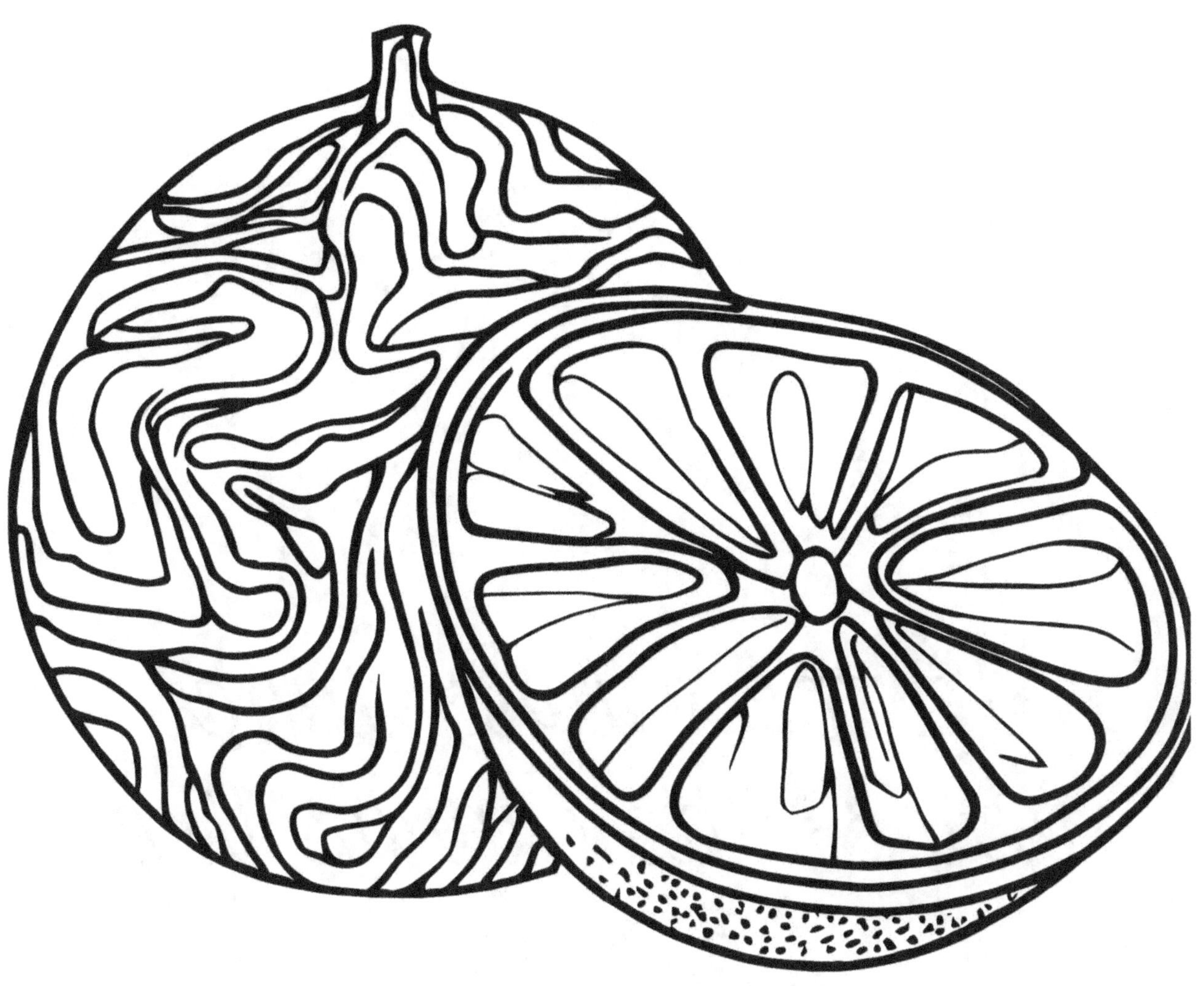

It is...

____

Let the colors dance across the canvas like poetry.

It is...
____

Painting is a journey
of self-expression and
discovery.

It is...

____

Unlock your inner artist and let your imagination run wild.

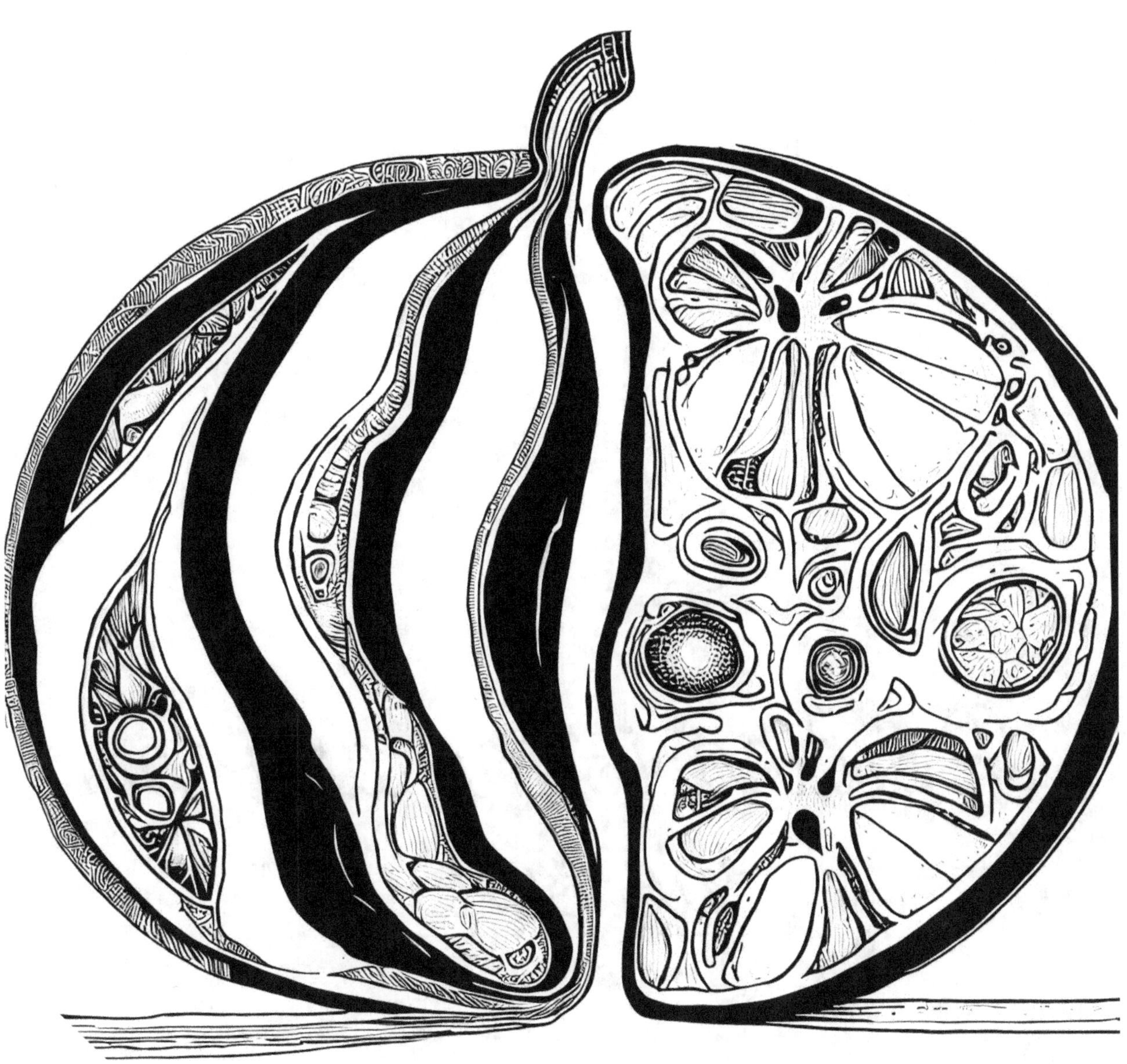

It is...

____

Painting is therapy for the soul.

It is...

____

Your brush is a magic
wand that brings
dreams to life.

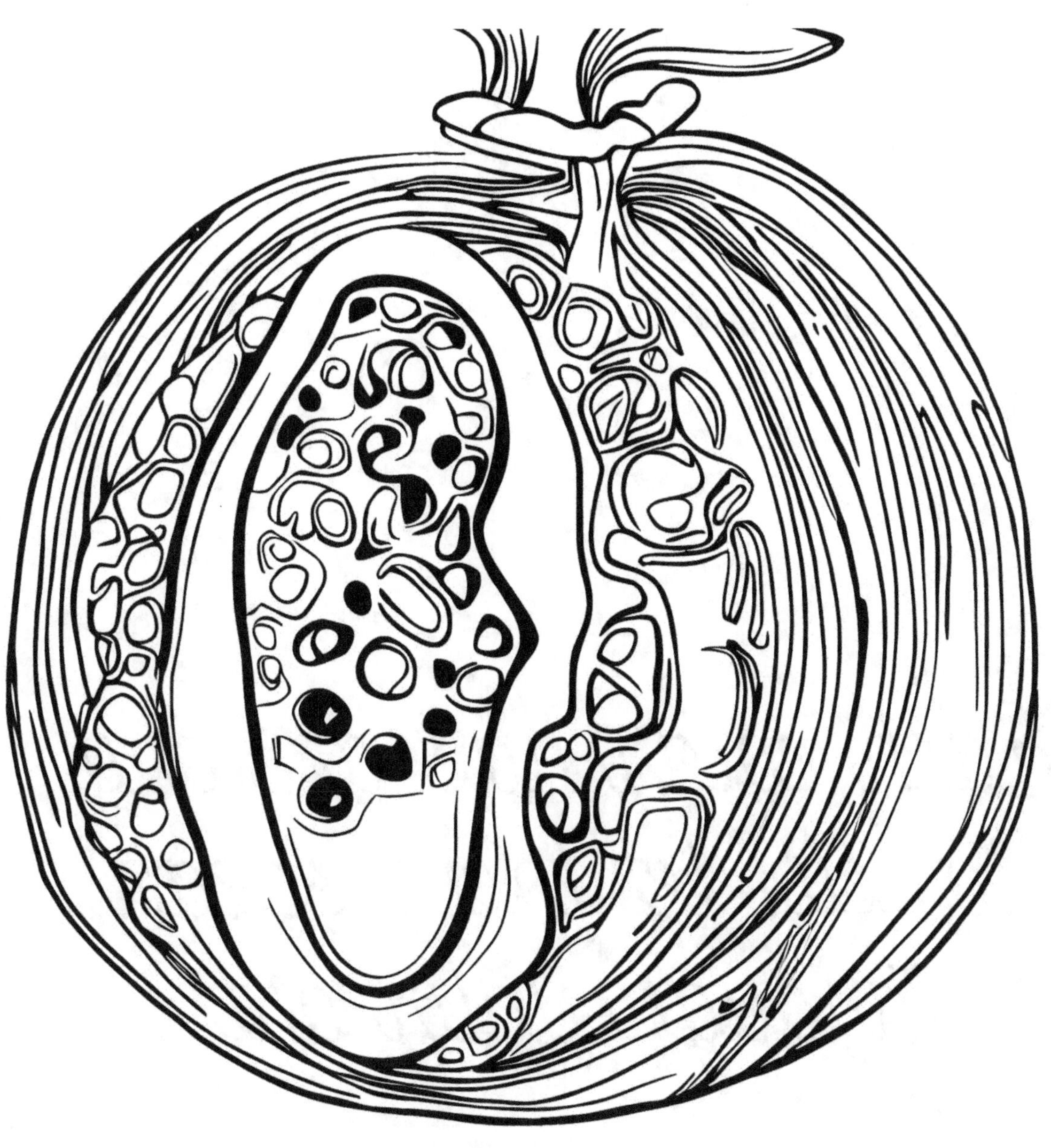

It is...

____

Each color has a story
to tell; let them speak
through your art.

It is...

____

Let go of worries and
find solace in the world
of colors.

Your face is familiar to me

Dive into the ocean of hues and let your spirit be refreshed.

It is...

____

Let your art be a reflection of the beauty within you.

It is...

____

Painting is a language
that transcends words.

It is...

____

Embrace imperfections
and celebrate the
uniqueness of your art.

It is...

____

Painting is a
sanctuary where your
mind finds peace.

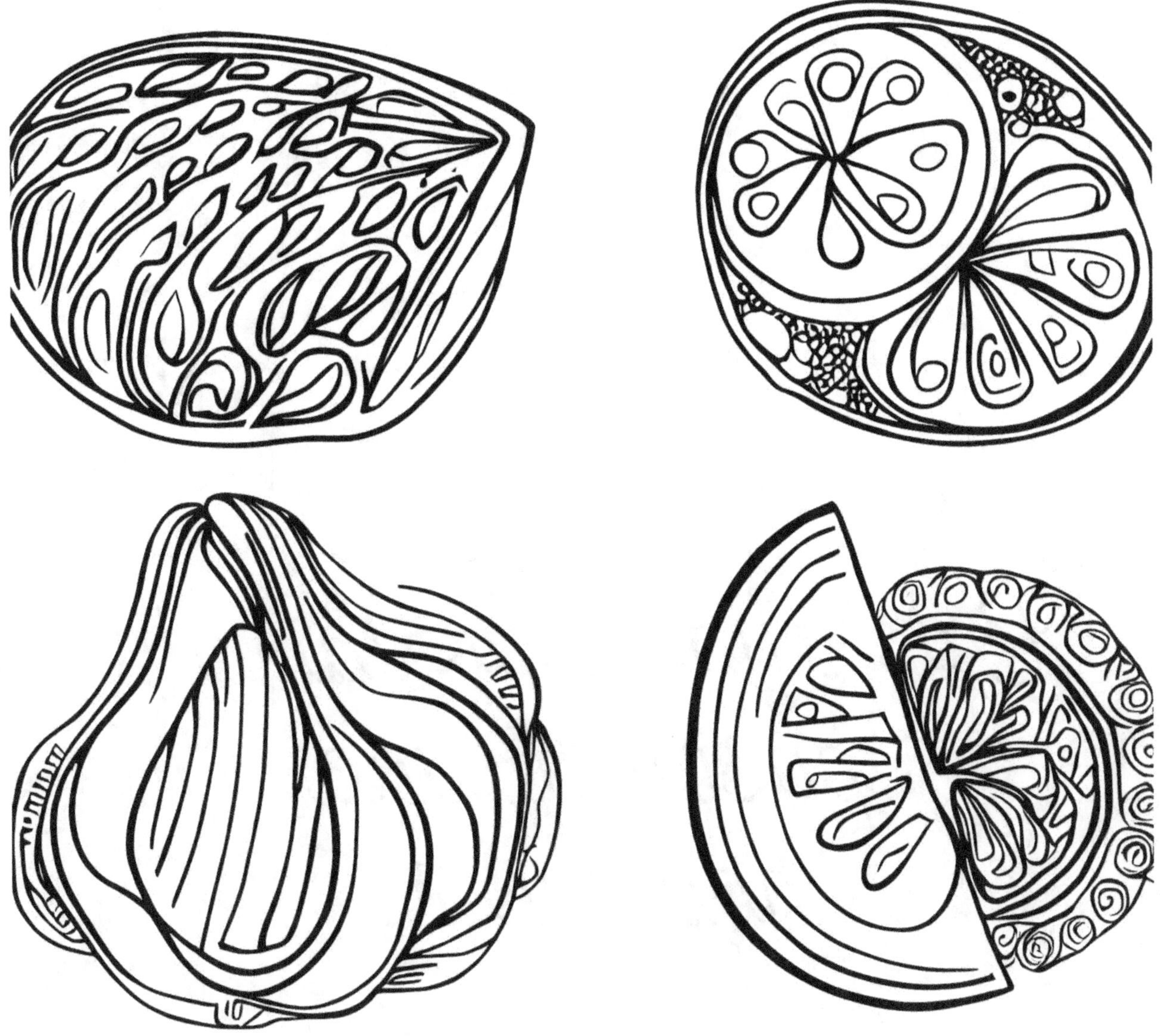

It is...

____

Color your world with positivity and happiness.

It is...

____

In the realm of art,
you are the creator of
your own reality.

It is...

____

Let your brushstrokes tell a story that words cannot express.

It is...

____

Find inspiration in the colors of nature and let them guide your hand.

It is...

____

Your art is an expression of your innermost thoughts and emotions.

It is...

____

Painting allows your heart to speak without words.

It is...

____

With every stroke, you release a little piece of your soul.

It is...

____

Unleash the artist within and let your creativity shine.

It is...

____

Embrace the blank
canvas as a world of
endless possibilities.

It is...

____

The act of painting is a form of meditation for the mind and soul.

It is...

____

Let the colors breathe life into your imagination.

It is...

____

Through art, you can create your own reality.

It is...

____

Allow the colors to heal and uplift your spirit.

It is...

____

Painting is a celebration of your unique perspective on the world.

It is...

____

Let your art be a reflection of your inner strength and resilience.

It is...

____

With each stroke, you add a little more beauty to the world.

It is...

____

Embrace the freedom that comes with expressing yourself through art.

It is...

____

Painting is a gateway
to a world of infinite
possibilities.

It is...

____

Let the colors on your palette be your guide to self-discovery.

It is...

____

Allow your art to be a mirror that reflects the depths of your soul.

It is...

____

Painting is an escape from reality into a world of endless beauty.

It is...

____

With each brushstroke, you create a symphony of emotions.

It is...

____

Let your art be a testament to the beauty that exists within you.

It is...

____

Let the brush be an extension of your soul, expressing emotions too deep for words.

It is...

____

Painting is a journey of self-discovery and self-expression; let it unveil the beauty within you.

It is...

____

With every stroke, let your emotions flow onto the canvas, creating a masterpiece of feelings.

It is...

____

Allow the act of painting to be a cathartic release, freeing your mind from worries.

It is...

____

Immerse yourself in the world of colors and let them spark your imagination.

Your face is familiar to me

Find solace in the art of painting and let it uplift your spirit.

It's time to create your own fruit, follow the pattern. Remember that dreaming and painting means reality!

Congratulations for coming here. I
hope this book gave you everything
you expected.

To be continued..